GIG JOBS IN

HIGH-TECH

by Heidi Ayarbe

BrightPoint Press

San Diego, CA

BrightP⬦int Press

LIBRARY OF CONGRESS CATALOGING-IN-PUBLICATION DATA

Names: Ayarbe, Heidi, author.
Title: Gig jobs in high-tech / by Heidi Ayarbe.
Description: San Diego, CA: BrightPoint Press, [2023] | Series: Exploring
    jobs in the gig economy | Includes bibliographical references and index.
    | Audience: Grades 10-12
Identifiers: LCCN 2022008617 (print) | LCCN 2022008618 (eBook) | ISBN
    9781678203887 (hardcover) | ISBN 9781678203894 (eBook)
Subjects: LCSH: Technology--Vocational guidance--Juvenile literature. |
    Temporary employees--Juvenile literature. | Gig economy--Juvenile
    literature.
Classification: LCC T65.3 .A93 2023 (print) | LCC T65.3 (eBook) | DDC
    602.3--dc23/eng/20220405
LC record available at https://lccn.loc.gov/2022008617
LC eBook record available at https://lccn.loc.gov/2022008618

CONTENTS

AT A GLANCE

- Gigs are short-term, temporary jobs.

- Gig workers are also known as independent contractors or freelancers.

- The gig economy boomed in the late 2000s and continued to grow after the 2020 COVID-19 pandemic.

- Companies are now relying on gig workers more than before. High-tech gig workers give companies opportunities to innovate and grow.

- High-tech gig jobs include computer programming and website development. Other roles include artificial intelligence (AI) engineers, virtual reality programmers, concert techs, and even drone pilots.

- There are many online platforms for high-tech gig workers to find work or advertise their skills.

- The Internet of Things (IoT) is the network of objects connected to the internet. This includes everything from home security systems to smart watches. Many high-tech gig jobs relate to the IoT.

DRONE SHOWS AND HIGH-TECH GIG WORK

"Drones launching. Five, four, three, two, one. Drones away."

Ximena gazed up and held her breath. More than a year of work was finally coming together for a seven-minute show. Ximena had arrived at Dollywood Theme Park just a few days before. Dollywood is in the Smoky

Dollywood is a theme park owned by singer Dolly Parton.

Mountains in Tennessee. It's known for its

music, rides, and nighttime fireworks show.

A fleet of 400 Intel Shooting Star 3

drones zipped to the sky above. The drones

People can use drones to create different images in the night sky.

looked like fireflies. They blinked in the

night sky.

The drones formed a spiral. The night

sky turned black for just a few seconds.

Then the drones formed more shapes.

They made a boom box, stars, a rising sun,

hearts, and human figures. Each image was

timed perfectly to music. The show ended with part of Dollywood's logo. It was a butterfly fluttering its wings.

Then each drone returned to the launch pad. An eruption of applause filled the air. The crowd whistled and cheered. Ximena exhaled.

Ximena and her three crewmates had spent the last two days preparing for this moment. They unloaded more than 7,000 pounds (3,175 kg) of gear. They checked the drones, their batteries, and their propellers. The crew had to set up and maintain the 400 drones in the show.

There are many uses for drones. In addition to light shows, drones can be used for filming, photography, exploration, or recreation.

After the show, they picked up all the

equipment. They stored it safely it in a shed.

It was a long day, and they had to get ready

for another show tomorrow. Dollywood's

Summer Celebration would last much

of the summer. The crew had a total of

thirty shows to do. Ximena felt proud and tired. She was part of something new. Her work involved creativity, problem solving, innovation, and some heavy lifting.

EXCITING OPPORTUNITIES

Ximena is a high-tech gig worker. A gig is a one-time job. Gig workers are also known as independent contractors or freelancers. People in the gig economy work a wide variety of high-tech jobs. Web designers create websites for businesses. 3D printer technicians build everything from small toys to entire houses. Drone operators help put together amazing shows in the night sky.

And skilled hackers help companies find problems in their computer security.

Not so long ago, these were jobs of science fiction. In the future, new jobs will emerge that haven't even been imagined. Technology is a key piece of just about every field and company today. High-tech workers are in high demand. The world of high-tech gig work is a dynamic and exciting field.

Many industries rely on workers with technical skills in order to run smoothly.

CHAPTER ONE

THE HISTORY OF GIG JOBS IN HIGH-TECH

Though it experienced a boom in the mid-2000s, gig work isn't new. Throughout history, artisans, craftsmen, and seasonal agricultural workers provided specific services. Many were gig workers.

By the 1800s, goods began to be produced by machines. Many people moved to cities to work in the factories.

One of the earliest gig jobs was traveling from farm to farm to work for short periods of time. Some people still work this way.

They left farms and rural life behind. Over time, the way people worked changed. They tended to keep the same job for a long period of time. This traditional work model continued for many years.

Throughout much of the 1900s, people often worked the same job for many years.

Louis Hyman is a historian of work and business. He writes, "Americans wanted security and stability pretty much more than anything."[1]

Changes in the world and technology brought gig work back. In the 1940s, temp agencies started to form. These companies would hire workers for tasks such as typing. They would then send the workers to other businesses to do that task for short periods of time. By the 1990s, nearly 10 percent of Americans were independent contractors or temporary workers.

THE REBIRTH OF THE GIG ECONOMY

In the late 1990s and early 2000s there was a boom in technology. This affected people's everyday lives. In 1984, only 8 percent of households had a home computer. By 2007, 69 percent of homes had a personal computer. Technology became more affordable as well as more powerful.

The internet also helped grow the gig economy. In 2000, less than 7 percent of the world had access to the internet. By 2021, more than 50 percent of the global population was online. As the internet spread, so did easier access to gig work. In 1995, the website Craigslist was created. Craigslist allows users to post ads. Users can buy or sell items online. They can also post job opportunities. Many people began using Craigslist and similar websites to find gigs.

Early personal computers were often clunky. They had far less power than today's computers.

Along with the growth of the internet came the birth of social media. Myspace was one of the first social media sites. In 2004, it had 1 million monthly users.

As of 2021, Facebook was the most popular social media site in the world.

The use of social media exploded. By September 2021, there were almost 3 billion monthly Facebook users. More than 1 billion people used Instagram. About 1 billion used TikTok. Social media and the gig economy grew together. Social media allows gig workers to show off their skills. Employers can use social media to look for workers who meet their needs.

In September 2008, the US stock market crashed. Many people lost their jobs. The economy was in a **recession**. At the recession's height, 10 percent of people were out of work. People began calling this period The Great Recession. The recession ended in 2009, but the economy took years to recover.

After losing their jobs, many people turned to gig work. Some were unable to find traditional jobs. Others didn't feel that a traditional job was a good fit for them. Gig work helped people pay their bills. After the recession ended, many people returned to traditional jobs. Others continued to work gigs.

WOMEN AND HIGH-TECH GIG WORK

Women are underrepresented in high-tech jobs. A 2020 study revealed that women held only about 25 percent of computing jobs. The gig economy might be changing this. Because of the gig economy, women can set their own hours and work from home. Women often have more responsibility for caring for children than men. Gig work gives them flexibility many traditional jobs don't. Gig work also gives women access to high-tech jobs. They can reshape their roles in the workplace.

THE WORK-FROM-HOME MOVEMENT

The internet opened many work possibilities. Email and telecommunication made work more flexible. People could work from home. Companies could hire people from around the world. Some high-tech gig workers can work from almost anywhere in the world. They include programmers and web designers. Others, like drone operators, are hired and travel to specific gigs.

Daniel Masata worked as a senior vice president at Adecco Engineering and Technology. He saw a change in the way

Many people prefer working from home. They may have more flexibility to care for their families.

high-tech workers wanted to work. He says

that in 2005, 75 percent of candidates

looking for technology jobs at his company

wanted full-time jobs. By 2015, that number dropped to 50 percent.

When the COVID-19 pandemic hit in 2020, many people worked from home to avoid catching the disease. Many tech companies, including Facebook, Twitter, and Google, announced that some employees could work from home permanently. Other companies, such as Microsoft and Apple, announced they wanted employees to resume working in person. Some people switched to gig work to have more flexibility.

THE INTERNET OF THINGS (IoT)

The **Internet of Things** (IoT) is a collection of devices that connect to the internet. Smart watches, home security systems,

THE IoT AND SOFT DRINKS

One of the first examples of the IoT comes from a vending machine. In the early 1980s, Coca-Cola had a modified vending machine at Carnegie Melon University. It was connected to an early version of the internet. Lights in the machine indicated if a row was empty. The lights would turn off when the machine was refilled. So students wrote a computer program. The program would check to see if lights were on. If the lights were off, the program would say how long ago the machine had been filled. Before getting a soda, people would connect to the network. They could check to see if there were drinks available and if they were cold.

and more are all part of the IoT. IoT devices have become a big part of people's lives. This has created more work for gig workers in technology. In 2018, the number of tech jobs in the United States grew by 200,000. More high-tech workers are needed to meet the demands of the changing world.

Steven Girouard is a program manager at Intel Drone Light Shows. He says that he has seen a change in the way his organization hires and works with gig workers. In the past, temporary workers were hired to work full time for several months at a time. This mirrors a traditional work schedule.

Now it's more common to hire gig workers who get paid by the job. Girouard explains, "The advance in computing technology, internet speeds, and most recently, the work-from-home movement has made significant advances. . . . I think gig work is here to stay."[2]

The work-from-home movement allows workers to do their jobs from anywhere. Many freelancers choose to travel.

CHAPTER TWO

WORKING A GIG JOB IN HIGH-TECH

Many tech workers are drawn to gig work. They can work with many types of businesses. They have the freedom to choose their projects. Many different tech jobs can be done as gigs. Some jobs are one-time projects. Other jobs are short-term contracts. This gives workers flexibility to choose what works best for them.

Many different types of tech jobs are suited to gig work.

TECH BEHIND THE SCENES

Eric Hillman works for the band 311. Some

people call him a roadie. Roadies have

always been part of the gig economy.

They work with bands and traveling

entertainment. But there's been a big

Concert techs often have a lot of electronic gear they must set up and maintain for bands.

change in their responsibilities over

the years.

Hillman is responsible for setting up

and maintaining some of the band's

technical gear. This includes setting up amplifiers and pedals for the bass player and guitarist. He ensures effects devices have fresh batteries. Hillman runs sound checks before a show to make sure the equipment is working properly. During a concert, he manages a soundboard.

He works behind the scenes to make sure the show comes off without a hitch. Sometimes frequencies from nearby airports and military bases can disrupt the wireless microphones and amps. A big part of his job is fixing problems quickly. "So many things run wirelessly that people

A lot of equipment used in a concert is wireless. Techs must make sure the devices work correctly so fans don't miss part of the music.

don't realize that the simple interruption of

a signal could be a drop out of the show,"

Hillman explains.[3]

Hillman also runs social media for the band. He manages the Instagram tour page, posting content from the band. He posts everything from behind-the-scenes moments to concert highlights. This helps the band connect with fans.

His days are long. He often wakes up on a bus, traveling with the band. The job is hard, but Hillman loves it.

WORKING ON WEBSITES

Jen Rolston works in digital marketing. She designs and develops websites for businesses. She has worked with more than 600 clients. Rolston first began doing gig work in 2000. She chose to freelance because she wanted a flexible work schedule. That way she could spend more time with her children. She also wanted time for her hobbies.

She studied photography and computer graphics in college. The software programs she uses to develop websites didn't exist back when she graduated in 1994. She is mostly self-taught.

César Giraldo is a high-tech gig worker from Colombia. He began in the field in the early 2000s. When his family fell on hard times, he taught himself how to design

Web developers create websites for people and businesses. Many web developers are gig workers.

websites. He first developed a website to

rent his family's farm to travelers. This was

before most tourist places even had their

own websites. He loved to travel and paid for his trips by creating websites in places he visited. He says it was hard to convince businesses that websites were important. He was persistent and traveled the world selling his tech services.

Giraldo's work has evolved. He is now a search engine optimization (SEO) specialist. An SEO specialist is someone who works to increase the number of people who visit or use a website. A person does this by making the website easier to find on search engines such as Google. Giraldo helps businesses improve their websites.

SEO specialists adjust websites to try to maximize the number of visitors.

This includes changing the website's page design and content. Giraldo has worked with organizations around the world.

Giraldo says, "A well-positioned website is the difference between having a beautiful inviting store on Main Street compared to having one in a dark, back alley, next to smelly dumpsters, with crime-scene tape all over it."[4]

KEEPING PERSONAL DATA SAFE

Almost everything can be done online now. Banking, checking grades, applying for

THE GOOGLE SEARCH

For a website to be successful, ranking high in Google is important. Google is the most popular search engine. More than 90 percent of searches are made on Google. In 2021, there were an estimated 63,000 searches per second. For a website to be successful, it must do well in Google search results. SEO specialists know how to boost a website's ranking.

jobs, and shopping happen online. People give out highly personal information online every single day. This information may include their name, birth date, address, phone number, credit card number, and more. When people give this personal information to well-known companies, it's usually safe.

This safety often comes from the work of **ethical** hackers. A hacker is a person who is an expert at breaking into computer systems. Some people use their hacking skills for illegal activities. They may steal people's data, damage companies, or shut down equipment. Other hackers use their knowledge to defend against criminal hackers. Ethical hacking is a growing type of gig work. The hackers work with all kinds and sizes of organizations. This includes hospitals, government agencies, banks, and more. Their job is to break into a computer system or network. It's like hiring a skilled thief to steal a bank's money. The thief finds flaws and weaknesses in security. Hiring ethical hackers is a way for organizations to improve their cybersecurity. This helps keep people's data safe.

FINDING GIG WORK

Part of being a successful gig worker is marketing yourself. There are also many online job sites. Gig workers must actively pursue **leads**. This means they look for work opportunities. Some leads can be

GIG PLATFORMS

There are many online platforms that gig workers can use to find work. Often, the gig worker must **bid** on a job. That means they say how much money they're willing to do the job for. Not all leads end up in paid work. Rejection is a big part of gig work. When a gig worker gets a job, the platform takes a percentage of the gig worker's income. Some popular platforms for gig workers are Toptal, Upwork, Freelancer, Fiverr, and Guru.

found on the internet. Others come from word of mouth. This is when businesses or customers recommend a worker to new customers.

Successful gig workers aim to improve their skills. They also have to be good at pursuing opportunities. They develop a good reputation in their industry. They are known as being flexible, hard-working, competent, and reliable.

Gig workers must constantly search for new work opportunities.

CHAPTER THREE

PROS AND CONS OF GIG JOBS IN HIGH-TECH

Working a high-tech job in the gig economy has its ups and downs. Gig work isn't for everybody. It can be challenging. Some key parts of traditional work aren't easily available to gig workers. Likewise, the traditional model of work isn't for everybody. Some people don't like the idea of going to the same place for work

*Gig work comes with many benefits.
However, workers must balance those against
the drawbacks.*

every day. Others want to choose their

projects. It's important to understand the

advantages and disadvantages of gig work.

THE PROS OF HIGH-TECH GIG WORK

There are many advantages to being a high-tech gig worker. Flexibility is one. Gig workers have more flexibility in the hours they work and where they work. They also have more flexibility in the jobs they want to take. Erik Kennedy is a computer programmer. He left a traditional job at Microsoft to do gig work as a programmer. Kennedy says, "I wanted a little more freedom and was willing to take a little more risk."[5]

Gig workers must manage their time to get work done. But they can often choose

Gig workers can often set their own schedules. Instead of working traditional office hours, a gig worker may choose to work in the evening.

their location. Some work from home, while

on vacation, or at their favorite cafés.

Another perk of gig work is that it can

be easier to get into. Many full-time jobs

require college degrees. But gig work often

requires only skills and experience. For example, a concert tech should know about musical instruments and how concerts work. He or she may not need a degree. To operate a drone, there are courses to become a drone service provider.

SKILLS FOR SUCCESS

Besides having technical skills, gig workers need **soft skills**. Self-discipline and initiative keep successful gig workers actively learning, looking for work, and meeting deadlines. Strong communication is key to understanding the needs of employers and reporting back to them. Flexibility and adaptability are important to adjust to new work environments and demands. A successful gig worker is an entrepreneur, manager, and employee all at the same time.

César Giraldo got a college degree related to agriculture. Everything about his SEO work has been self-taught. Giraldo says, "I spend a lot of time on websites and blogs to learn about . . . how to improve search engine optimization for my clients. Learning is one of the most important parts of my job."[6]

Gig workers also benefit employers. Mike Volkin is an instructor of an online class for freelancers. He says that organizations benefit the most from the gig economy for one clear reason: talent. He writes, "Quality talent is the single biggest contributor to a

Many traditional jobs offer health insurance, retirement savings programs, or paid time off. Gig workers have to find other ways to pay for these.

company's success. In the gig economy,

instead of having access to talent in your

geographic area, companies can now

access highly specialized talent anywhere in

the world."[7]

THE CONS OF HIGH-TECH GIG WORK

Most traditional full-time jobs come with
benefits. Benefits can include health
insurance, dental care, and sick time. They
may also include paid vacation, retirement
savings plans, and more. Most gig workers
do not receive these benefits. They have
to pay for these things themselves. If gig
workers get sick, they often do not get
paid. As of 2021, 80 percent of full-time
gig workers said they would have trouble
paying an unexpected bill.

Gig work isn't always reliable. This means
gig workers can spend a lot of time looking

for jobs. They must find ways to manage money without knowing when their next job will come in. Many leads don't end up in paid work. Sometimes companies need to cut costs. They often eliminate gig positions first.

If a gig worker doesn't work, she doesn't get paid. This means gig workers are constantly looking for new customers. Jen Rolston, a website developer, says one of the biggest challenges of gig work is not getting burned out. The insecurity of gig work can be stressful.

The process of seeking out new work can be time-consuming.

Identity and loneliness are two

issues many gig workers struggle with.

Sometimes gig workers feel disconnected

from the organization that hires them.

Many freelancers struggle with feeling isolated. Connecting with coworkers or other gig workers can help ease these feelings.

They don't have the chance to get to know other employees.

Sometimes traditional employees don't trust gig workers. Other employees may think gig workers don't work as hard.

This can make it even harder for a gig worker to feel connected. He or she might not experience a sense of community at a workplace.

STARTING A SIDE GIG

Gig work doesn't have to be the only kind of work someone does. Some people enjoy doing both gig work and having a traditional job. They develop a side gig. This is sometimes called a side hustle. It is often based on a hobby or interest. These side gigs can grow to become a main job.

Starting a side gig is a way to expand skills. Side gigs can also diversify income.

Many people became unemployed due to the COVID-19 pandemic. Some of them turned to gig work.

This means a person doesn't count on only one source of income. This can be very important in uncertain times.

Between 2000 and 2021, the United States saw multiple recessions. One was in 2008. Another was in 2020. Many people lost their jobs. Because of these recessions, more people began to do gig work for extra income. Sometimes this was in addition to

FROM SIDE HUSTLE TO MULTIBILLION-DOLLAR BUSINESS

Steve Jobs and Steve Wozniak are the founders of Apple. Jobs worked the night shift at Atari. It was a leading video game company in the 1970s and 1980s. Wozniak was an engineer at a computer company named Hewlett Packard. In their free time, they built a computer in a garage out of Atari parts. They called it the Apple I. They later formed the company Apple. In 2021, Apple made nearly $95 billion.

their traditional work. Other times it was to replace a traditional job.

Kimberly Palmer is a personal finance expert and author. She encourages people to start side gigs. She says, "It's so easy to launch a side gig today. If you have an inkling for something you might want to do, just get started."[8] Someone with an extra income source is better prepared for the unexpected. And a side gig may eventually become a full-time work opportunity.

There are many benefits to having a side gig. The extra money can be used to pay off expenses or build savings.

CHAPTER FOUR

THE FUTURE OF GIG JOBS IN HIGH-TECH

The gig economy is growing three times faster than the traditional workforce in the United States. It is projected that by 2027, 86.5 million workers in the United States will be gig workers. A key piece of this growth is technology. There are many different ways tech workers can participate in the gig economy.

Project-based gigs last only until a project is completed. This includes work such as designing a website, improving a website's SEO, or developing an app.

HIGH-TECH GIG WORK AND THE PROJECT ECONOMY

Project-based work is a big part of the gig

economy. This is when someone is hired

to complete a specific task or project.

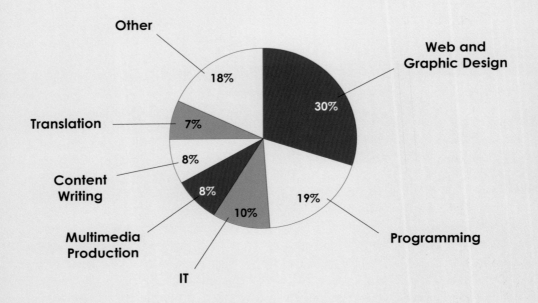

MOST POPULAR FREELANCE CAREERS

Other — 18%

Translation — 7%

Content Writing — 8%

Multimedia Production — 8%

IT — 10%

Web and Graphic Design — 30%

Programming — 19%

Source: "The 2020 Freelancer Income Report," Payoneer, n.d. https://pubs.paynoeer.com.

A 2020 report from finance site Payoneer broke down the most popular freelance gig jobs. The top three careers were all in the tech industry.

Project-based work may involve hiring a

programmer to write code for a video game.

It might be hiring a web developer to create

a website. Intel hires gig workers for specific

drone light shows like the Dollywood Summer Celebration.

Project-based work is good for both gig workers and organizations. Companies can hire workers for short periods of time. This gives gig workers flexibility. The gig workers can take jobs based on their interests and passions.

Andrew Burke is the dean of Trinity Business School. He says that project-based gig work is key to organizations growing, diversifying, and improving. High-tech gig workers allow organizations to try new things.

Organizations who hire gig workers have access to highly specialized skills for specific needs. Hiring a gig worker for a short period of time is not as expensive as hiring a traditional worker.

TRENDS TO LOOK OUT FOR

Technology has changed how businesses work. It has changed the way organizations communicate and operate. It has changed security systems and allowed people to work from home and find jobs online. Technology has improved efficiency and business operations. Behind all of this technology are high-tech workers.

Many IT workers take short contracts with businesses.

As the gig economy grows, there

are trends to watch. In 2018, the ten

highest paying gig jobs were in tech.

These roles included artificial intelligence

(AI) programmers, robotics freelancers,

and ethical hackers. Some of the most in-demand gig jobs in 2021 include IoT engineering and mobile app development.

CREATIVE DESTRUCTION

Creative destruction is a term invented by the economist Joseph Schumpeter in 1942. He used it to describe changes in technology that replace old ways of doing things. One of the biggest examples of creative destruction is the internet. Travel agents lost work because people began to make hotel and airplane reservations online. Bookstores closed because people started buying books online. Though many jobs were lost because of the internet, even more jobs were created. These included high-tech jobs for programmers, web developers, and more.

THE FUTURE IS NOW

Many young people see gig work as a common career. Can Erbil is a professor of economics at Boston College. He believes gig work is appealing for young workers. He says, "We now have a generation of workers who never had full-time jobs."[9]

It's estimated that around 9 million people lost their jobs in the United States by the end of 2020. The economic crisis came from the COVID-19 pandemic. But economic crises bring forward new ideas and new ways to do business. This is called creative destruction. In 2020, more than 4.4 million people began their own

businesses. This was up 24 percent from

3.5 million in 2019.

Sarah Hinawi is the founder of a

consulting organization called Gig Economy

PROTECTIONS FOR GIG WORKERS

Many companies save money by hiring gig workers. They often don't offer benefits such as sick leave or vacation time to gig workers. However, some people want to change that. When the COVID-19 pandemic hit, some cities began passing laws to protect gig workers. Gig workers who got sick from the disease could get sick pay. A federal law passed in March 2020 temporarily allowed gig workers to get unemployment pay. However, these benefits expired in September 2021. Many gig workers called for permanent protections.

Learning and Leadership (GELL). She has worked with young people around the country to help prepare them for the world of gig work. She says, "We are in a new world of work, and both individuals and organizations need to be thinking differently about what it takes to be prepared."[10]

Hinawi says that being skilled in technology isn't enough. Gig workers must be creative. They need to know how to consider risks. They must be able to handle failure. Often gig workers are rejected by possible customers. Successful gig workers must have strong communication skills.

And, more than anything, they must want to learn and grow as professionals.

The gig economy is always changing. As technology expands, the need for high-tech gig workers will grow. In 2010, many jobs that would be common a decade later didn't exist. By 2030, this field will likely include many new jobs most people haven't even imagined. The keys to success are to keep learning, continue growing, and stay curious. It's an exciting, dynamic future. Being a high-tech gig worker can open many opportunities.

The demand for tech workers is expected to increase in the near future. Many of these opportunities may be for gig work.

GLOSSARY

benefits

extra perks given by a company to a worker, besides pay

bid

to offer to do work for a job or project

ethical

following accepted and morally right rules of behavior

Internet of Things

the collection of devices that connect to computers and each other using the internet

leads

potential opportunities that gig workers find for new work

recession

when a country's economy goes through a difficult period

soft skills

personal skills that help someone better communicate with others

SOURCE NOTES

CHAPTER ONE: THE HISTORY OF GIG JOBS IN HIGH-TECH

1. Quoted in Meghana Chakrabarti, "The Origin Story of the Gig Economy," *WAMU*, August 20, 2018. https://wamu.org.

2. Steven Girouard, Personal interview, September 5, 2021.

CHAPTER TWO: WORKING A GIG JOB IN HIGH-TECH

3. Quoted in "How We Make a Living in the Gig Economy: Day in the Life Marathon," *CNBC Make It*, June 8, 2021. www.youtube.com.

4. César Giraldo, Personal interview, September 21, 2021.

CHAPTER THREE: PROS AND CONS OF GIG JOBS IN HIGH-TECH

5. Quoted in Tam Harbert, "Tech Pros Make the Most of the 'Gig Economy,'" *Computerworld*, September 8, 2015. www.computerworld.com.

6. César Giraldo, Personal interview, September 21, 2021.

7. Mike Volkin, "Why the Gig Economy Will Drive the Future of Employment," *Forbes*, March 27, 2020. www.forbes.com.

8. Quoted in Christine Ryan Jyoti, "7 Ways to Start a Successful Side Gig," *Fast Company*, March 28, 2014. www.fastcompany.com.

CHAPTER FOUR: THE FUTURE OF GIG JOBS IN HIGH-TECH

9. Quoted in Tam Harbert, "Tech Pros Make the Most of the 'Gig Economy.'"

10. Sarah Hinawi, "Ethos," *Sarah Hinawi*, n.d. www.sarahhinawi.com.

FOR FURTHER RESEARCH

BOOKS

A. W. Buckey, *Gig Jobs in Social Media*. San Diego, CA: BrightPoint Press, 2023.

Sheryl Normandeau, *Become a Web Developer*. San Diego, CA: BrightPoint Press, 2023.

Reshma Saujani, *Girls Who Code: Learn How to Code and Change the World.* New York: Puffin, 2018.

INTERNET SOURCES

Monica Anderson, Colleen McClain, Michelle Faverio, and Risa Gelles-Watnick, "The State of Gig Work in 2021," *Pew Research Center,* December 8, 2021. www.pewresearch.org.

Amy Boyington, "Side Hustles for Teens – 20 Best Ways to Start Making Money Today," *Frugal for Less*, December 11, 2021. www.frugalforless.com.

Mary Clare Novak, "How Does SEO Work?" *G2*, January 11, 2021. https://learn.g2.com.

WEBSITES

BEANZ: The Magazine for Kids, Code, and Computer Science
https://kidscodecs.com

This website includes everything from articles about detoxing from social media to thoughtful use of technology.

PBS: Future of Work
www.pbs.org/wgbh/future-of-work/watch

This three-part series is about what work will look like in the future, touching on many high-tech topics.

Scratch
https://scratch.mit.edu

Scratch is a website that allows people to learn coding by creating and playing computer games.

INDEX

IMAGE CREDITS

ABOUT THE AUTHOR

Heidi Ayarbe is an author, translator, storyteller, and gig worker. She lives in Pereira, Colombia, with her family.